The P Diddy Case – From Mogul to Monster

Sophia Fairview

Published by Independent Artists Network, 2024.

While every precaution has been taken in the preparation of this book, the publisher assumes no responsibility for errors or omissions, or for damages resulting from the use of the information contained herein.

THE P DIDDY CASE – FROM MOGUL TO MONSTER

First edition. October 9, 2024.

ISBN: 979-8224311996

Written by Sophia Fairview.

Table of Contents

Foreword

Power and fame are intoxicating forces. They have the potential to inspire greatness and innovation, but in the wrong hands, they can also fuel exploitation, manipulation, and abuse. The world of **Sean "Diddy" Combs**—once the embodiment of success, glamour, and cultural influence—reveals just how quickly those lines can blur, and how devastating the consequences can be when unchecked power takes root.

In writing this book, I've aimed to explore the **dualities** that so often exist within public figures, particularly those like Diddy, whose persona became larger than life. Here was a man celebrated for his business genius, his impact on hip-hop, and his transformation from Harlem hustler to global mogul. But as the layers peeled back, another story emerged—one not of glitz and triumph, but of **control, abuse**, and lives left broken in the shadows of his success.

This story is not just about the downfall of a powerful man. It's a reflection of the broader industry and cultural dynamics that allowed such behavior to flourish for decades. Diddy's empire wasn't built in isolation—it thrived within a system that often enabled **misconduct** through silence, complicity, and the allure of celebrity. And while Diddy's story may be unique in its scope and visibility, it is far from an isolated case.

The tale you're about to read is difficult and, at times, disturbing. But it's also necessary. As we delve into the rise and fall of one of the most influential figures of our time, we must also confront our own roles in the systems that let men like Diddy ascend unchecked. **It's time for accountability**, not just for Diddy but for an industry that has long overlooked the pain it inflicted on those left in its wake.

This book aims to spark a broader conversation—about **power, abuse**, and how the world of entertainment can move forward with integrity. Because no matter how untouchable a person might seem, no one is above facing the truth.

Sophia Fairview

From Puff Daddy to Love: The Many Faces of Sean Combs

"**F**irst, he was Puff Daddy, then P. Diddy, then just Diddy, and now he's 'Love.' At this rate, we're one more name change away from him becoming a symbol, just like Prince!"

When it comes to Sean Combs, the name changes are almost as frequent as the scandals. Puff Daddy, P. Diddy, Diddy, and now Love. It's as if every time his image starts to get a bit too tarnished, he hits refresh with a new identity. But no matter how many times he reinvents himself, those shadows of controversy and whispered rumors are never far behind. From the flashy public persona to the darker, hidden stories, one thing is clear: behind the name changes lies a man who, for decades, has played the game of power, often at the expense of those around him.

Harlem Beginnings

THE EARLY STRUGGLES

Before Sean Combs became a global icon, he was just a kid from **Harlem**, New York. Born in 1969, Sean grew up without a father, who was murdered when he was only two years old—a tragedy that hung over his early life like a storm cloud. His mother, **Janice**, did her best to shield him from the harshness of the world, working tirelessly to provide, but Harlem in the 70s wasn't an easy place to raise a child.

From the beginning, Sean was taught to hustle. But Harlem wasn't just about ambition; it was about **survival**. And it's from those streets that Sean learned early on how to navigate both the legal and not-so-legal sides of life. His father's involvement in the drug trade was no secret, and though Sean would later claim he never went down that path himself, it's impossible to ignore how early exposure to this underworld might have shaped his understanding of power and control.

What's clear is that Sean's drive came not just from wanting success, but from a desire to escape the vulnerability he felt growing up fatherless in a neighborhood where violence was always a heartbeat away.

Hustle Mentality

Sean's hustle started young. By the time he was a teenager, he was already organizing parties that were the talk of the neighborhood. But here's where we begin to see the more manipulative side of Sean emerge. Even in high school, there were whispers that Puffy didn't just want to be successful—he wanted to **control**. He knew how to get what he wanted from people, and that was a skill he'd perfect as he climbed the ladder of fame.

By the time he reached **Howard University**, Sean wasn't just throwing parties—he was building connections, and, as some would later claim, stepping on anyone he needed to in the process. Howard was just a stepping stone, a place for him to make the right contacts, but not somewhere he saw himself staying long. He left after two years, convinced that the world outside was ready for him, and more importantly, that he was ready to take it.

But even then, the stories followed him: rumors of women being manipulated, of people being used and discarded once they no longer served a purpose. "While most of us were dreaming of our next holiday, young Puffy was probably dreaming of his next empire—and who he'd have to step on to build it."

The Big Break

Sean's big break came when he landed an internship at **Uptown Records**. But make no mistake, this wasn't your typical internship. Sean made it clear from day one that he wasn't there to learn—he was there to **take over**. And that's exactly what he did. He quickly rose through the ranks, producing hits for artists like **Jodeci** and **Mary J. Blige**, but it wasn't all smooth sailing.

Behind the scenes, there were rumblings. Sean was known for his temper, for being **ruthless** in business. Some called it ambition; others called it exploitation. There were rumors that he'd push artists to the breaking point, using them as stepping stones for his own success. And then came the more serious accusations—those involving manipulation and coercion, particularly when it came to women.

In 1993, Sean was **fired** from Uptown Records, reportedly due to his **aggressive behavior.** But some insiders suggest it wasn't just about his temper—it was about what was happening behind closed doors. There were whispers that his firing had less to do with business disagreements and more to do with the way he treated people, especially women.

And this was just the beginning of a pattern that would follow him for the rest of his career: using power, influence, and fear to get what he wanted. "Nothing says 'I'll show them' quite like founding a multimillion-dollar record label—especially when you've left a trail of burned bridges behind you."

Sean Combs might have rebranded himself countless times, but the whispers of scandal and the darker stories never disappeared. Whether it was the rumors of coercion and abuse that haunted his early years or the power plays that defined his rise, one thing is clear: each new name wasn't just a reinvention—it was an attempt to bury the past. But no matter how many times you change your name, the truth has a way of resurfacing.

Bad Boy Records and Beyond: Shaping 90s Hip-Hop

DOMINATING THE 90S Music Scene

The Golden Era of Hip-Hop

By the mid-90s, **Bad Boy Records** had become synonymous with success. It wasn't just a label; it was an **empire** that pumped out hit after hit, shaping the sound of an entire generation. If you weren't blasting Bad Boy artists like **Mase**, **Faith Evans**, or, of course, **The Notorious B.I.G.**, you weren't just out of the loop—you were missing the very pulse of 90s hip-hop.

Combs knew how to put together a roster of talent that could dominate the airwaves and clubs alike. Bad Boy's artists didn't just rap—they created anthems. And while the West Coast had its G-Funk vibe, Bad Boy owned the East Coast, cranking out tracks that had everyone nodding their heads and singing along. It was the golden era of hip-hop, where every new release felt like a cultural moment.

And honestly, back in the 90s, if you weren't listening to a Bad Boy artist, were you even cool?

The Shiny Suit Era

Ah, yes—the **shiny suit phase**. Let's take a moment to appreciate it, shall we? Picture it: Diddy, decked out in a reflective, **glitzy suit**, bouncing across the screen in music videos that were more like short films. It was an era defined by **over-the-top excess**, and no one did excess quite like Diddy. The flashy suits, the **explosive choreographed routines**, the helicopters—it was all part of the fantasy Diddy was selling, and let's face it, we all bought into it, at least for a while.

Admit it—you tried the shiny suit dance in front of the mirror at least once... and failed miserably.

But beyond the fun and ridiculous outfits, the shiny suit era represented a bigger trend in hip-hop at the time: the **mainstreaming of luxury**. Hip-hop was no longer just a gritty underground scene; it was entering the pop culture stratosphere, and Diddy was at the helm, steering the ship with all the glitz and glamour he could muster.

The Production Powerhouse

THE P DIDDY CASE – FROM MOGUL TO MONSTER

What set Diddy apart from other moguls was his ability to turn the art of music production into an unstoppable machine. **Sampling** was his secret weapon—taking classic hits from the past and giving them a modern twist that made them instantly recognizable yet fresh. And it worked. **Every time**.

Diddy had a way of blending the old and the new, creating songs that stuck in your head and refused to leave. His production style wasn't just catchy—it was radio gold. Every beat, every hook, every bass line was engineered to **make you move**, even if you didn't want to. Let's be real—he had a way of making you nod your head, whether you wanted to or not.

But beneath the gloss of success, there were murmurs of something darker. Stories circulated about the pressure he put on artists, the **contracts that weren't as golden as the hits**, and the feuds that seemed to follow him like a shadow. The shiny suits were blinding, but the cracks beneath were becoming harder to ignore.

Creating a Lifestyle Brand

Sean John

Diddy wasn't content with just being a music mogul. He wanted to shape how people **lived, dressed**, and **celebrated** success. In 1998, he launched **Sean John**, his clothing line that would go on to become a **cultural phenomenon**. And while you might chuckle at the idea of a rapper designing high-end suits, Sean John wasn't a joke—it was the real deal, embraced by celebrities, athletes, and everyday folks alike.

Nothing says 'I've made it' quite like wearing a suit designed by a rapper.

Sean John wasn't just about clothes; it was about selling a **lifestyle**. The brand stood for luxury, success, and, of course, a certain level of **swagger** that was unmistakably Diddy. Whether it was the oversized leather jackets, the velour tracksuits, or those infamous **suits**, Sean John wasn't just a fashion label—it was a statement. If you were wearing Sean John, you were part of the elite, or at least that's what Diddy wanted you to believe.

Cîroc and Revolt TV

But why stop at clothes? Diddy had bigger plans. He wanted to be in every aspect of your life—right down to what you drank and what you watched. Enter **Cîroc** vodka, one of the smartest business moves of his career. He didn't just endorse the brand; he made it his own, turning it into a household name. Suddenly, Cîroc was the vodka of choice at every party, every club, and every VIP event. If you were celebrating, you were doing it with Cîroc.

You know you've reached the top when you're not just throwing parties—you're the one selling the vodka and broadcasting the party on your own TV network.

And then there was **Revolt TV**—Diddy's foray into media, where he wasn't just shaping music anymore; he was shaping the entire conversation around it. Revolt TV was his attempt to **control the narrative**, to give hip-hop its own platform, free from the mainstream networks. It was bold, ambitious, and, in true Diddy fashion, all about **power**.

Music Videos We Can't Forget

Iconic Videos

When we talk about Diddy's legacy, we can't forget his **music videos**. These weren't just videos—they were events. Big-budget, cinematic productions that dripped with **luxury**, **style**, and the kind of excess that made you wonder, *Is this a music video or a Hollywood blockbuster?*

There were helicopters, yachts, extravagant mansions, and of course, Diddy himself, dancing in every scene, looking like he owned the world (because, in his mind, he probably did). These videos were designed to make you feel like you were part of the good life, that champagne-soaked vacation you never knew you wanted.

The helicopters, the yachts, the furs—Diddy's videos made you think every day was a champagne-soaked vacation... unless you were the guy holding the camera.

Cultural Impact

Diddy's videos didn't just sell music—they sold a **lifestyle**, one that every aspiring artist and fan wanted a piece of. He made **luxury** feel accessible, or at least, aspirational. If you couldn't afford it, you could at least **dream it**, and those dreams were inescapable when you watched his videos.

The **bling culture**, the **excess**, the **sunglasses indoors**—somehow, Diddy made it all feel normal. He took the **hip-hop aesthetic** and polished it until it glittered, making even the most outrageous outfits and behaviors seem like the height of cool. *Somehow, he made us believe that wearing sunglasses indoors was perfectly normal.*

But as with everything Diddy touched, beneath the surface was always a sense of **control**, of power that wasn't easily relinquished. The man who built an empire from nothing wasn't just selling music or clothes or alcohol—he was selling a piece of himself. And for a long time, the world couldn't get enough.

The Charm and Charisma: Public Persona vs. Private Reality

THE FACE OF BAD BOY

Diddy the Showman

If there's one thing Sean Combs mastered early on, it was how to make **Bad Boy Records** more than just a label—it became a **cultural movement**. And a large part of that came down to Diddy's larger-than-life persona. He wasn't just the guy behind the artists; he was **the artist**, the businessman, the man who could be anywhere and everywhere all at once. He knew how to get people talking, how to stay in the spotlight, and, most of all, how to make everything feel bigger than life.

Take, for instance, his infamous **White Parties**—those exclusive, star-studded affairs where everyone, and I mean **everyone**, from Hollywood to hip-hop, was dying to get an invite. Who else could throw a party so big, they gave it a color theme? Enter, the White Party... which was just an excuse for celebrities to get together and pretend they're not all hungover. But, it worked. The world ate it up. It was part of the allure—**the glitz, the glamour, the exclusivity**.

But of course, parties were just a part of the show. Diddy knew how to work a crowd, whether it was at a glitzy event or hosting the **MTV Video Music Awards**, where his charismatic, smooth-talking persona made him seem untouchable. To the public, Diddy was the ultimate showman. And for years, no one questioned it. Why would they? He wasn't just hosting a party; he was hosting an **era**. And we all bought a ticket.

Public Image vs. Reality

But here's the thing about those larger-than-life personas—they're often the perfect cover. The bigger the show, the more dazzling the lights, the more we forget to look at what's happening behind the scenes. Diddy's public charm wasn't just charisma—it was **armor**. A shield. The man was always smiling, always in control, always giving the world exactly what it wanted to see.

But, as with most things in the world of celebrity, **the bigger the smile, the bigger the shadows it can hide**.

Behind the flashy suits, the VIP parties, and the champagne, there was always another story—a darker one. Diddy's charm was his weapon, and he wielded it with precision. In public, he could win over anyone, but **what happened behind closed doors?** That's where the real Diddy lived, and as rumors would have it, that Diddy wasn't always so charming.

The Power of Charisma - Winning Over the Public

THE P DIDDY CASE – FROM MOGUL TO MONSTER

Diddy's greatest strength wasn't just his business acumen or his knack for making hit records. It was his ability to **win people over**. From fans to executives, from artists to fellow celebrities, Diddy had an almost magical ability to make you believe in him, even if you didn't quite know why. He could light up a room, throw the best party, and leave you feeling like you were part of something special, even if you were just an extra in his grand show.

And that was his genius. He didn't just sell music; he sold **a dream**. Whether it was the glittering image of success he crafted around Bad Boy Records or the countless parties and events he orchestrated, Diddy made sure that when you thought of him, you thought of luxury, power, and charm. He didn't just host a party; he hosted an era. And we all bought a ticket.

Keeping Up Appearances

But here's the thing about **charisma**—it's often the perfect tool for distraction. It's easy to keep people looking at the glitz and the glamour when you don't want them focusing on the cracks beneath. For years, Diddy's charm was enough to keep the public—and the media—focused on his success, his wealth, his ever-growing empire.

But **was it all just part of the act?** And if so, how long does the curtain stay closed before the real story sneaks out?

Because no matter how charming someone is, no matter how perfect they seem in the spotlight, **the truth has a way of finding its way through**. And with Diddy, the whispers of something more sinister were always just below the surface. There were always **rumors**—about how he treated people, about what went on behind the scenes at Bad Boy, about the lengths he would go to maintain his empire.

Duality of Celebrity - The Dark Side of Fame

One thing you quickly learn in the world of celebrity is that there's always a **duality**—the public persona and the private reality. For Diddy, that duality was extreme. On stage, in interviews, at events, he was the charismatic, unflappable mogul who had it all together. But **behind closed doors**, it seemed there was another man entirely.

It's the age-old question: *"Is it the person we see on stage? Or the one behind closed doors that really counts?"* With Diddy, the difference between the two was staggering. Publicly, he was generous, charismatic, the life of the party. Privately, there were stories—dark stories—about manipulation, control, and even abuse. Over the years, those whispers grew louder, but no one wanted to hear them. **Hints of Trouble: After all, who wants to spoil the party?**

But if you looked closely, there were always **hints of trouble**. Behind the charm, behind the smiles, Diddy wasn't just a businessman with a plan—he was someone willing to do whatever it took to get what he wanted. Those close to him often spoke of his **manipulative tendencies**, of how he'd charm you one minute and destroy you the next if you crossed him. It wasn't just business—it was personal.

As the empire grew, so did the **rumors**. People whispered about the contracts, the way artists were treated, the **control** Diddy exerted over everyone in his circle. Behind the flashy façade was a man obsessed with power. And maybe all that glitz wasn't just blinding us—it was hiding something far darker.

As we close this chapter on Sean Combs, it's impossible not to marvel at the sheer **audacity** of his journey. From Harlem to Hollywood, from Puffy to Love, he didn't just chase success—he **created** it, built it, and wrapped it in shiny suits and champagne bubbles. He was never content with just being another player in the game. He wanted to **own** the game. And for a while, it seemed like he did. The man wasn't just a musician or a businessman; he was a **spectacle** in every sense of the word.

But, as with any spectacle, the lights eventually dim, and we're left wondering what happens **behind the scenes**. As much as Diddy mastered the art of public charm, there's always another story lurking in the shadows—the whispers, the rumors, the cracks in the foundation that are impossible to ignore.

Because in the world of Sean Combs, **success wasn't just about making music**—it was about creating a spectacle. **But behind every spectacle, there's always a backstage story waiting to be told.** And sooner or later, that story always comes to light.

The Cracks Beneath the Surface

Feuds and Altercations: The Realities Behind the Public Drama

On the surface, Sean "Diddy" Combs' **public feuds** often seemed like typical entertainment industry drama—artists clashing over business, ego, or creativity. After all, hip-hop has long thrived on rivalry, and fans are used to seeing stars engage in public disputes. But what looked like ordinary spats in the media were often far more insidious beneath the surface. These altercations weren't just about **competitive tension**—they were manifestations of a deeper, darker pattern of **control, intimidation, and manipulation.**

Take, for instance, the infamous **feud with rapper Kid Cudi**. In 2012, Diddy's jealousy over Cudi's growing closeness to his then-girlfriend, Cassie Ventura, reportedly boiled over into something far more sinister. According to legal documents, Diddy allegedly **threatened to blow up Kid Cudi's car**, a threat that soon materialized when Cudi's car mysteriously **exploded in his driveway**. This was no mere coincidence. Kid Cudi later confirmed the explosion through his representatives, adding a chilling layer to what had seemed like a petty celebrity argument. It was a sharp reminder that when Diddy felt threatened, he didn't just argue—he **destroyed.**

But as explosive as that feud was, it's just the tip of the iceberg compared to Diddy's private life. His **long-term relationship with Cassie Ventura**—the woman at the center of the Cudi feud—was filled with far more disturbing incidents. In 2023, after years of silence, Cassie came forward with a **lawsuit detailing years of abuse**. Her claims were shocking, outlining not only **physical violence** but an atmosphere of constant emotional and psychological manipulation that left her trapped for nearly a decade.

One of the most disturbing incidents occurred in 2016, when a violent argument in a Los Angeles hotel spiraled out of control. Diddy, in a fit of rage, was captured by **hotel security cameras** as he **dragged Cassie through the hallways** and **threw vases** at her as she desperately tried to escape. For years, this footage was hidden from public view. According to court documents, Diddy allegedly paid **$50,000 to hotel staff** to suppress the video, ensuring that it never made the news. But, like many dark secrets, it eventually surfaced, and the world finally saw a glimpse of the violence Cassie had endured behind closed doors.

Cassie's lawsuit didn't just focus on that single incident. She detailed a long pattern of abuse—emotional, physical, and sexual. For years, she was coerced into situations she wanted no part of, including what Diddy called **"freak-offs"**—wild, drug-fueled parties where she was forced to engage in sexual acts with other men while Diddy watched. Cassie's account painted a grim picture of a woman trapped by Diddy's **manipulative and controlling** nature, unable to escape because of the immense power he wielded.

It wasn't just Cassie who felt the brunt of Diddy's wrath. Numerous other former employees and associates have come forward with similar stories of **intimidation, coercion, and physical violence**. One of these individuals, **Rodney "Lil Rod" Jones**, a producer at Bad Boy Records, claimed he was repeatedly **harassed, drugged, and physically assaulted** by Diddy during their time working together. Jones' accusations echo the same pattern of **control and manipulation** that Cassie described, showing that Diddy's behavior wasn't confined to romantic relationships—it extended into his professional life as well.

Diddy's **violent outbursts** weren't isolated incidents; they were part of a larger strategy of **fear and dominance**. Those around him quickly learned that crossing Diddy—whether in business, personal relationships, or even casual interactions—could have dire consequences. This wasn't just about ego; it was about **maintaining power**. Many who worked with or for Diddy have spoken about the **climate of fear** he cultivated, where people were too scared to speak out or push back, knowing that doing so could end their careers—or worse.

For years, Diddy was able to hide these behaviors behind his public image. His charm, charisma, and undeniable business acumen made it easy for the public to focus on his achievements, rather than the growing number of **whispers and rumors** about his darker side. **Bribery and intimidation** were key tools in keeping his worst actions out of the spotlight. When things did slip through the cracks—like the **hotel security footage** of him assaulting Cassie—Diddy's immense wealth and connections allowed him to **cover up or suppress** the truth, paying off victims and buying silence where needed.

But as more and more victims come forward, a much clearer picture of Diddy's behavior is emerging. What was once dismissed as celebrity drama or industry rivalry is now being seen for what it truly was: **a systemic pattern of abuse**, power plays, and a dangerous mix of fame and violence. His empire, built on talent and charisma, is now being revealed to have been propped up by **intimidation, manipulation, and cruelty**. And as the walls around him continue to crumble, it's becoming impossible to separate the mogul from the **monster** lurking beneath.

The public feuds, once seen as mere industry gossip, are now pieces of a much larger and more sinister puzzle. Diddy's violent tendencies, his need to **dominate and control** those around him, were not just the cost of doing business—they were the foundation of his entire empire. And as these cracks in his carefully constructed façade continue to widen, the question remains: *How much of this empire was built on the suffering of others?*

One thing is clear—the charming, charismatic Diddy we saw on stages and red carpets was only half the story. Behind the **glitzy suits** and **million-dollar smile** was a man willing to destroy lives, all in the name of protecting his own power. And now, finally, those stories are being told.

Manipulation and Control: The Hidden Power Plays

WHEN IT COMES TO **manipulation and control**, Sean "Diddy" Combs' alleged tactics go far beyond the business realm. This wasn't just about ensuring his artists were loyal or that deals went his way—**control** for Diddy, it seems, was something far more personal, and, disturbingly, **systematic**. His power didn't just reside in his wealth or his influence within the music industry—it extended into the most intimate corners of people's lives, and for those trapped in his orbit, escape wasn't easy.

For years, Diddy's former girlfriend, **Cassie Ventura**, recounted the level of **coercive control** she endured, painting a picture that reads less like a bad relationship and more like a nightmare. Cassie wasn't just **emotionally manipulated**; she was allegedly forced into sexually exploitative situations, under the guise of fulfilling Diddy's **voyeuristic fantasies**. These weren't just wild nights of partying—they were **carefully orchestrated "freak-offs,"** where Cassie and others were coerced into engaging in sexual acts with male prostitutes while Diddy watched. And this wasn't some low-key affair—according to Cassie, Diddy often filmed these acts, all while distributing drugs like candy to ensure everyone was "compliant" enough to follow through with his demands.

Imagine that: the man who sells vodka by the bucketload is also doling out **cocaine and methamphetamine** like party favors—not to amp up the fun, but to keep his **victims compliant**. And while everyone was dazed and under the influence, Diddy sat back and recorded the chaos, under the pretense of "fun." Cassie, like many others, was left to **disassociate**, trapped by the drugs and the power imbalance, knowing that refusing to participate could mean even greater consequences.

But Diddy's control didn't end with Cassie. As more accusers step forward, a clear **pattern of manipulation** emerges. It wasn't just about parties or sexual exploitation—it was about **power**. The consistent thread running through each story is Diddy's **ruthless need to dominate**. Whether through drugs, violence, or his sheer financial might, Diddy made sure everyone knew who was in charge. His **empire**, it seems, was not built on music alone, but on a complex system of **coercion**—a web so tight that those caught in it feared speaking out, even years after their encounters.

To add another layer of dark irony to this, **Diddy's wealth** wasn't just a shiny reflection of his success—it was a weapon. In an industry where financial power is often the key to silence, Diddy wielded his riches like a sword. For those unfortunate enough to find themselves on the wrong side of his temper or whims, speaking out wasn't an option. How could it be? They were up against a man who could pay off security footage to keep his crimes hidden, who could **financially ruin careers** with a single word, and who had the **media in his back pocket**. What's a lawsuit against a billionaire? It's a whisper in the wind.

But whispers, it turns out, have a way of growing louder. And as more victims come forward, Diddy's house of cards begins to wobble. These aren't just isolated incidents of bad behavior. No, they're **decades of abuse**, carefully managed and systematically covered up. The drug-fueled parties, the threats, the coercion—it all points to something more than the misdeeds of a man who let fame go to his head. What we're seeing now is the unmasking of someone who didn't just use power—he **abused** it, over and over again.

Perhaps the most chilling part of these allegations is how **calculated** they are. This wasn't someone caught up in the moment, losing his temper during a heated argument. Diddy allegedly orchestrated these moments of control, ensuring that every victim was trapped not just by the situation, but by their own **helplessness**. He provided the drugs, he held the camera, and he sat at the center of a toxic web, watching as his victims were pulled further into his **sphere of influence**.

For the longest time, people wondered how someone like Diddy, who appeared so polished in public, could hide such horrors behind the scenes. But that's the nature of true **manipulation**—it's not just about what you do in private. It's about the **image you project**. And Diddy's image was always one of **success, charm, and control**. The reality, however, is far darker.

In the end, the question remains: *Was Diddy's empire built on charisma and business savvy, or on a foundation of **fear, manipulation, and control**?* For those who've been brave enough to speak out, the answer is all too clear.

Fame and Power: The Cost of Success

WHEN WE THINK ABOUT the heights Sean "Diddy" Combs has reached in his career, it's easy to get lost in the **glitz and glamour**. Here's a man who defined a generation of hip-hop, who became synonymous with success, luxury, and power. But as more allegations emerge, painting a far darker picture, we're forced to reconsider: *How much of that success was built on talent? And how much on fear and control?*

At the heart of this question lies a troubling **duality**. On one hand, Diddy has long been celebrated as a charismatic mogul, the face of Bad Boy Records, an empire that reshaped music in the 90s and early 2000s. He was charming, magnetic, the kind of guy who could light up a room and leave everyone wanting more. Yet, as the stories from his past begin to unravel, another side emerges—one that shows a man far less concerned with charm and far more obsessed with **dominance**.

THE P DIDDY CASE – FROM MOGUL TO MONSTER

The accounts that have surfaced over the years—many coming to light after Cassie's explosive lawsuit in 2023—indicate that Diddy wasn't just a savvy businessman; he was someone who sought **absolute control**, both professionally and personally. The men and women who worked closely with him have painted a picture of an individual who didn't merely crave power; he **demanded** it. For Diddy, it wasn't enough to be at the top of the industry—he had to ensure that everyone around him knew who was in charge, whether through charm or, more disturbingly, **through intimidation and coercion**.

As we pull back the curtain on Diddy's empire, we begin to see how deeply ingrained this pattern was. The stories of **physical and emotional abuse**, of **drug-fueled parties** and **coercive sexual encounters**, aren't isolated incidents—they are part of a broader narrative. Diddy's success, it appears, wasn't just about the music or the business deals. It was about **control**—over the artists who worked for him, the women in his life, and anyone else who threatened to step out of line.

This isn't just speculation. The testimonies of those who've come forward in recent years paint a chilling portrait of a man who **systematically** used his power and influence to get what he wanted, no matter the cost to those around him. As more accusers speak out, including both men and women, we begin to see the extent of this manipulation. Many feared retribution, knowing full well that Diddy's influence could end their careers—or worse. The pattern of **fear and silence** that he allegedly fostered is deeply troubling and suggests that his empire was as much built on **intimidation and exploitation** as it was on talent and business acumen.

And so, we're left with the uncomfortable question: *Was this simply the price of business in an industry rife with abuse, or was this business broken from the start?* It's no secret that the entertainment industry has long shielded powerful men from accountability, allowing them to engage in **dark behaviors** while hiding behind fame and fortune. Diddy's story forces us to confront that reality head-on.

What's most striking is the **duality** of his persona. Publicly, Diddy has always been the **charming mogul**, the life of the party, the king of the hip-hop world. But privately, as these allegations suggest, he was someone else entirely—someone capable of **terrifying abuse and manipulation**. For years, this duality worked to his advantage. His public face was so carefully constructed, so well-maintained, that few were willing to look deeper. But now, as the stories begin to pile up, it's clear that the charming Diddy we knew was only part of the story. Behind the scenes, there was a man whose quest for control left a trail of **victims** in its wake.

As the walls around him continue to crumble and the truth comes to light, we are forced to reconsider what it means to be successful in the world of fame and power. Diddy may have built an empire, but it's an empire that, as we now know, was propped up by **manipulation, coercion, and fear**. It's a sobering reminder that in the world of celebrity, what glitters on the surface often hides the darkest of secrets.

In the end, we have to ask ourselves: *How much of this success came at the cost of others' suffering?* Because as more stories emerge, one thing becomes abundantly clear—Sean Combs didn't just build a music empire. He built a **spectacle**, and like any great spectacle, there's always a backstage story that the audience wasn't meant to see.

The Dark Side of the Parties

MOST OF US THINK WE know what celebrity parties are like: champagne flowing, luxury everywhere, and a guest list straight out of a movie premiere. But when you pull back the curtain on **Diddy's "Freak Off" parties**, you find a much more disturbing reality. These weren't the glamorous, high-end affairs that you might imagine when you think of a hip-hop mogul living it up. Instead, these events involved **drug-fueled orgies, violence**, and **sexual exploitation**, all carefully controlled and orchestrated by Diddy himself. The stories that have emerged over the years show just how far from "fun" these parties really were.

THE P DIDDY CASE – FROM MOGUL TO MONSTER

At first glance, the idea of a celebrity party seems like a dream. But the **"Freak Off" parties** were nightmares disguised in wealth. The setting was always perfect: Diddy's sprawling mansions, luxury cars lining the driveway, the finest drinks, and a guest list of **handpicked women**. But these women weren't invited to dance or have fun—they were there for something much darker. According to multiple accounts, Diddy used **cocaine**, **GHB**, and **oxycodone** to **disorient and subdue** the women, ensuring their compliance for what was to come. The drugs weren't just casual party favors—they were tools of control, meant to break down resistance and **strip away any sense of autonomy** the participants might have had.

Once the drugs took effect, the **real horrors** began. **Diddy himself allegedly orchestrated the sexual acts**, watching from the shadows while women, often disoriented and scared, were forced to engage in acts with **paid male prostitutes** or other guests. This wasn't about indulgence or pleasure—it was about **power**. The acts were often filmed, sometimes with hidden cameras, and the footage was reportedly kept for **blackmail purposes**. This way, Diddy could ensure that his guests—and his victims—wouldn't speak out. The cameras were always rolling, not to capture memories but to **capture control**.

One of the most disturbing elements of these parties was the **coercion** involved. Many of the women didn't realize what they were walking into when they accepted an invite to one of Diddy's gatherings. Some were drawn in with promises of career opportunities or romantic attention. Once inside the mansion, however, they quickly realized they were **trapped**. Reports tell of **underage girls** being lured in, as well as women who had been in Diddy's orbit for years, either too frightened or too powerless to refuse his demands. In one particularly shocking account, a woman recalled how she tried to leave one of these parties, only to be **physically restrained** by Diddy's security guards. As she ran toward an elevator, Diddy himself chased her down, stopping her escape with a terrifying **glare of anger and power**.

The parties weren't just about sexual control—they were **performance art for domination. IV fluids** were allegedly kept on hand to help partygoers recover from the physical toll of the night's events, making it clear that these "freak-offs" weren't normal social gatherings, but highly controlled, drug-induced orgies designed to break down boundaries and reinforce Diddy's status as the one in charge. The lavish setting, the drugs, the forced performances—it all worked together to create an environment where the guests were **puppets**, and Diddy pulled all the strings.

But Diddy didn't operate alone. These events required **complicity** from those around him—**assistants, bodyguards, and even business associates**—all of whom played roles in ensuring the parties went off without a hitch. The same people who helped plan and execute these events were often responsible for keeping the details quiet. How much of it was done out of loyalty, and how much out of **fear**, is unclear. But one thing is certain: Diddy wasn't the only one profiting from these nights of horror. The people around him helped build a **wall of silence**, ensuring that the dark side of these "freak-offs" remained hidden for years.

What's particularly chilling about these events is the **length of time** they occurred. For over a decade, these parties happened in secret, with very few people knowing the truth. Those who did know were often **terrified into silence**—whether through financial coercion, threats, or the weight of Diddy's influence in the entertainment industry. These weren't one-off mistakes or moments of weakness. This was a **system**, carefully constructed and ruthlessly maintained.

It's one thing to hear stories about wild celebrity parties, but it's something else entirely to hear about events like this. Diddy's "Freak Off" parties show a man who wasn't just seeking pleasure or thrills—he was seeking **complete control** over everyone in the room. These stories are reminders that sometimes, the line between celebrity and **predator** is thinner than we think.

Coercion Behind Closed Doors

WHAT HAPPENS BEHIND closed doors, particularly in the world of the rich and powerful, often stays there—hidden beneath layers of **fear, silence, and control**. This was the case with Sean "Diddy" Combs' infamous parties, where, according to several disturbing reports, women weren't just attending wild celebrity events—they were **trapped**. These women weren't guests, they were **victims**, coerced and manipulated into participating in degrading acts through a **web of threats, drugs, and psychological manipulation**.

The allegations paint a deeply unsettling picture of how Diddy allegedly used **substances like ketamine and GHB** to keep women compliant. These aren't just party drugs; they're substances that impair a person's ability to think, resist, or even comprehend what's happening. **GHB**, in particular, is notorious as a "date-rape drug," often rendering individuals vulnerable and disoriented. Once these women were under the influence, they became pawns in Diddy's **disturbing games of power**.

Reports suggest that once the women were incapacitated, they were coerced into engaging in **degrading sexual acts**, often while Diddy watched. This wasn't about pleasure—it was about **control**. In many cases, these acts were **filmed**, sometimes without the participants' knowledge. The recordings allegedly served a sinister purpose beyond gratification: they were **used as blackmail**. These tapes weren't just trophies for Diddy; they were tools to **silence** the women, ensuring that they wouldn't speak out about what had happened.

But the real question here is: *How does this happen, and no one says anything?* For years, this calculated abuse of power flew under the radar, protected by Diddy's wealth, influence, and the **culture of fear** he cultivated. Those involved were often too terrified to speak out. After all, how do you fight a man with the **financial means** to bury the truth, and the **connections** to ruin your life if you dare to try?

The women involved were subjected to **psychological manipulation** as much as physical coercion. The threat of retaliation hung over them, creating a **chilling environment** where refusal wasn't an option. Many were led to believe that **their careers, reputations, and even their safety** depended on going along with Diddy's demands. Over time, this culture of control became a well-oiled machine, designed to keep victims isolated and afraid, while maintaining the illusion of consent.

This pattern of manipulation and control was not a one-time occurrence—it spanned **over a decade**, according to multiple allegations. Diddy's actions weren't impulsive; they were part of a **calculated abuse of power**. The women were systematically **isolated**, not just physically but emotionally, leaving them with nowhere to turn and no one to confide in. Those in Diddy's orbit were trapped in a cycle of fear, unable to escape the powerful man at the center of it all.

The real tragedy here is that these women, who thought they were walking into professional or romantic opportunities, were instead walking into a carefully constructed **trap**. Once inside, there was no easy way out. What started as a simple invitation to a celebrity event quickly turned into a **nightmare**, with their voices silenced, their autonomy stripped away, and their experiences hidden from the world behind layers of **secrecy and shame**.

For too long, this calculated abuse went unnoticed—protected by the very system Diddy had created. The combination of **drugs, threats, and manipulation** ensured that his victims remained compliant, while the world outside saw only the charming, successful mogul. But now, as more victims come forward, the truth is beginning to emerge, and we're left to ask: *How many lives were damaged or destroyed to protect the empire Diddy built?*

These weren't just bad decisions made in the heat of the moment. They were part of a **systemic pattern of exploitation**, designed to maintain **absolute control** over those who found themselves within Diddy's reach. And the more we learn, the clearer it becomes: this was no ordinary abuse of power—it was a **calculated, sustained assault on the autonomy and dignity of countless victims**.

The Role of Associates

WHEN IT COMES TO DIDDY'S **associates**, the question isn't just *what did they do*—it's *why did they do it?* Were they motivated by **loyalty**, or was it simply **fear** that kept them quiet? After all, maintaining silence while witnessing the horrors of these so-called "freak-off" parties couldn't have been easy, unless there was something larger at play. Maybe it was both—loyalty to a man who held so much power over their careers, but also **fear** of the consequences that would come with crossing someone like Diddy. He wasn't just a boss—he was a **gatekeeper** to the industry, a man with the ability to elevate or destroy careers with a snap of his fingers.

Diddy's **assistants, bodyguards, and close associates** allegedly played crucial roles in the orchestration of these twisted events. They weren't just running errands or fetching drinks. No, these individuals were reportedly responsible for **setting up the spaces**, ensuring the right guests were in attendance, and even **providing the drugs** that fueled the chaos. Some might have been acting out of obligation, simply doing what was expected of them. Others? Perhaps they were **complicit**, caught up in the cycle of power and excess, or maybe they were just as trapped by Diddy's dominance as the women he manipulated.

Turning a blind eye is something people are good at when the alternative is far worse. For many of these associates, turning against Diddy would likely mean **losing everything**—careers, reputations, and even personal safety. After all, Diddy wasn't known for handling disloyalty with grace. The same man who allegedly **threatened to blow up Kid Cudi's car** over a personal spat wasn't someone you'd want to cross. So, were they protecting their jobs, or were they protecting themselves? That's the question that lingers.

It's easy to wonder, *why didn't they speak up?* But when you realize the stakes—**the consequences of standing up to someone as powerful as Diddy**—it becomes clearer why silence might have seemed like the only option. These enablers were likely as much **prisoners of Diddy's power** as anyone else, carefully walking the line between doing what was asked and keeping themselves out of the crossfire. The more you hear about how these events unfolded, the more you understand that Diddy wasn't operating alone. He had a whole team of people making sure everything ran like a well-oiled machine, and each cog in that machine had a role to play. But at what cost?

Some might argue that these associates were **victims of circumstance**, caught in a system of exploitation themselves. After all, if you work for someone long enough, especially someone as powerful as Diddy, **you learn the rules.** You learn what's expected of you, and more importantly, you learn what happens if you step out of line. Others, however, might see them as **complicit**, aiding and abetting Diddy's behavior without ever challenging the horrors they witnessed. **Fear and power** are potent tools, and Diddy wielded both with deadly precision.

These "Freak Off" parties pull back the curtain on a side of **celebrity culture** that's difficult to comprehend. They weren't about indulgence or decadence—they were about **power, control, and exploitation.** And while the parties themselves might seem shocking enough, what's even more disturbing is how many people it took to make them happen. These weren't isolated events—they were part of a **system**, with Diddy at the helm, pulling all the strings.

It's one thing to imagine the high life of celebrities—lavish parties, expensive champagne, and fancy cars—but **baby oil and IV fluids to recover from drug-fueled orgies?** That's a reality check no one asked for. The stories that have surfaced show us just how far Diddy went to maintain his grip on power, using his influence not just to manipulate and abuse, but to ensure that no one—**not even his closest associates**—would ever dare challenge him. The more we learn, the clearer it becomes: these parties weren't just about excess—they were about **domination**, and Diddy stood at the center of it all.

Diddy's Criminal Network: The Combs Enterprise

When you think of **Bad Boy Records** and **Combs Enterprises**, you might picture hit records, sold-out shows, and an empire built on savvy business moves. But as it turns out, Diddy's business empire wasn't just about music—it was allegedly a front for something far more sinister. According to various indictments, Diddy used his corporate influence not just to make hits, but to **facilitate a highly organized criminal enterprise**. This wasn't your garden-variety celebrity scandal—this was an empire that allegedly thrived on **racketeering, sex trafficking, and drug distribution**.

Bad Boy Records wasn't just the birthplace of hip-hop legends—it became the perfect cover for Diddy's operations. Using his vast influence, Diddy allegedly lured victims under the pretense of **romantic involvement** or promises of **career advancement**. The dangling carrot of fame and success was enough to bring people into his orbit, but once they were in, things took a much darker turn. What started as professional opportunities often led to coercion, as victims were drawn into his elaborate and exploitative "freak off" events—events that were organized with disturbing precision.

Diddy's criminal activities didn't happen in isolation—they were part of a **well-oiled machine**. Behind the flashing lights and celebrity aura was a network of staff, assistants, and **high-ranking associates** working to make sure the illegal side of Diddy's operations ran just as smoothly as his chart-topping hits.

Organizational Structure

RUNNING A CRIMINAL enterprise like this required more than just a few shady characters on the payroll—it needed an entire **support system**. From **assistants** to **security personnel**, Diddy's operation allegedly functioned with military-like precision. Each person had a role to play, and they weren't just setting up parties—they were ensuring that these events were **carefully controlled environments** where Diddy could manipulate and dominate his victims with impunity.

Let's start with the assistants. They weren't just there to organize Diddy's schedule or fetch coffee. These employees were reportedly **booking hotel rooms**, **stocking drugs**, and coordinating **travel arrangements** for the victims and sex workers involved in the "freak offs." It wasn't just about making sure Diddy's parties went off without a hitch—these assistants were allegedly **facilitating the logistics** of his crimes.

Then there were the **security staff**, who played a crucial role in maintaining control. Their job wasn't just to protect Diddy from external threats; they were there to **enforce the internal rules** of these events. If a victim tried to leave, it was the security team's job to **ensure that didn't happen**. If hotel staff or others began asking questions, it was security's role to **bribe or intimidate** them into silence. These weren't just bodyguards—they were **gatekeepers**, controlling who came in and out of Diddy's world of exploitation.

But it didn't end with the personal staff. High-level **business partners** were also allegedly involved, ensuring that the criminal activities were **masked by legitimate operations**. Diddy's empire was built in such a way that these criminal activities blended seamlessly into his professional world. Whether it was organizing travel, drugs, or payouts, these partners were essential in keeping the machine running smoothly, ensuring that **money flowed freely** while hiding the darker dealings behind the scenes.

A Network Built on Fear

ONE OF THE MOST DISTURBING aspects of Diddy's alleged criminal network was how it thrived on **fear and manipulation**. Victims were often isolated, both physically and emotionally, and left with no options to resist. And while Diddy's financial power allowed him to cut people off or blackball them in the industry, his **psychological manipulation** was equally powerful. By keeping those around him **financially dependent** or **professionally isolated**, Diddy ensured that anyone who might oppose him was too fearful to act.

Victims weren't the only ones trapped in this system—many of his employees likely felt the same. Some may have acted out of **fear of retribution**, knowing full well what could happen if they crossed a man as powerful as Diddy. For others, the allure of staying close to one of the most influential figures in music may have clouded their judgment. Either way, the **cycle of silence and complicity** became a hallmark of Diddy's operations. Those who worked for him weren't just enablers—they were part of a **tightly controlled network**, making it nearly impossible for the truth to come to light.

What we see here is the stark contrast between Diddy's **public persona** and the allegations that are slowly tearing down the facade. On one side, you have a charming mogul, a larger-than-life figure who seemingly built an empire out of talent and charisma. On the other, you have allegations of a man who allegedly used that empire to hide an intricate web of **exploitation, abuse, and coercion**.

This wasn't just a one-man operation. It was a carefully orchestrated system, built on fear, maintained by **loyalty or fear**, and hidden under layers of glamour and success. For years, it ran like a well-oiled machine, until the cracks began to show.

Methods of Control

DIDDY'S ALLEGED **methods of control** weren't the kind that involved overt, obvious threats—not at first, anyway. They were far more insidious, relying on a combination of **financial leverage, emotional manipulation**, and a culture of **isolation and fear**. Over the years, this intricate web of influence allowed him to create a powerful **empire of dominance**, where everyone around him—whether victims, employees, or business partners—found themselves trapped under his control.

Financial Leverage

ONE OF DIDDY'S PRIMARY tools of control was his **financial power**. Money talks, and in Diddy's world, it also silenced. Those who displeased him or refused to comply with his demands reportedly found their **careers cut short**. In the music industry, where access to success often depends on powerful gatekeepers, Diddy's ability to make or break careers was a weapon he allegedly wielded ruthlessly. **Artists and employees who crossed him** or tried to step out from under his control were swiftly dealt with. Some found themselves **blacklisted** from the industry altogether, their once-promising careers suddenly drying up.

But the control didn't stop at careers. Many of his victims were made financially dependent on him. By controlling their access to funds, Diddy ensured they were **trapped in his orbit**. Any resistance would be met with **legal and financial battles** they couldn't hope to win, leaving them **isolated and powerless** to escape. For those who tried to walk away, Diddy's financial influence was used as both a carrot and a stick—offering support when they played by his rules and stripping it away if they dared to defy him.

Emotional Manipulation and Isolation

BEYOND MONEY, DIDDY reportedly used **emotional manipulation** to maintain control. **Isolation** was a key tactic, with victims often cut off from family, friends, and other support systems. Some of Diddy's alleged victims found themselves in situations where they were **physically and emotionally isolated** from outside help, leaving them entirely dependent on him. Whether through **physical separation** or constant **emotional pressure**, Diddy created an environment where the people around him felt there was nowhere to turn for help.

The **psychological toll** this took on victims can't be overstated. Manipulated into believing that they had no escape, many of Diddy's victims allegedly became resigned to the situation, trapped in a vicious cycle of control. His **wealth and celebrity status** made it nearly impossible for these individuals to seek justice. Even if they did try to escape or speak out, **who would believe them?** This created a world where victims were **silenced by fear**, leaving them unable to break free from the control Diddy exerted over them.

Threats and Blackmail

WHILE THE **financial and emotional manipulation** kept many in line, for some, Diddy allegedly resorted to **direct threats**—both explicit and implied. **Threats were commonplace**, according to reports, reinforcing a constant **climate of fear** among those around him. Victims who didn't comply were allegedly reminded of the **consequences**—the end of their careers, or worse, physical harm.

One particularly disturbing element of Diddy's control was the use of **blackmail**. Many victims claim that Diddy **recorded their participation** in the infamous "freak off" parties, often without their knowledge or consent. These recordings were allegedly used as leverage, ensuring that anyone who thought about going public with their story was quickly reminded of what could happen if those tapes ever saw the light of day. The threat of having compromising footage released was a powerful deterrent, leaving victims with no choice but to stay silent.

In this world Diddy created, **control was total**. He wasn't just a powerful businessman or a successful artist—he was a **puppet master**, pulling the strings of those around him through a combination of wealth, fear, and manipulation. His empire, as the allegations suggest, was built not just on talent but on a **systematic exploitation** of the people he had power over. And while the parties, the hits, and the fame were public, the **underlying mechanisms of control** remained hidden for years, only now beginning to unravel.

Links to Music Industry Figures

DIDDY'S RISE TO POWER didn't happen in a vacuum. He wasn't just a mogul because of his musical genius or business acumen; he was **deeply embedded in the fabric of the music industry**, relying on high-profile **industry figures** to maintain his influence and, allegedly, his control over others. Executives like **Lucian Grainge** (CEO of Universal Music Group) and **Ethiopia Habtemariam** (Motown Records) have been connected to Diddy, both professionally and socially. There are reports suggesting that some of these powerful individuals may have had knowledge of Diddy's darker activities but chose to remain silent, either out of **self-preservation** or the knowledge that crossing Diddy could mean the end of their careers.

In an industry where power dynamics are often skewed in favor of the wealthy and influential, the allegations against Diddy suggest that he used his connections to **shield his behavior**. It wasn't just that people were turning a blind eye—many were allegedly **complicit in creating an**

environment where Diddy could continue operating without scrutiny. Executives who had the power to question his actions or distance themselves reportedly chose not to, perhaps out of **fear of retaliation** or because they were benefiting from their association with him.

At the many **high-profile events** that populated the industry's social calendar, Diddy's presence was a given. From award shows to private gatherings, these events often featured the same people—the ones who **knew** what was going on but were unwilling or unable to intervene. The **culture of silence** that permeates the entertainment industry is one of its most troubling aspects. When so much is at stake—reputation, money, careers—many choose to look the other way, rationalizing their inaction by telling themselves it's "not their business."

Even artists who had collaborated with Diddy or were part of his circle might have had **suspicions** about his behavior, but the fear of being **blacklisted** or having their careers derailed was enough to keep them from speaking up. And while some may have had genuine loyalty to Diddy, believing he was simply **eccentric** or misunderstood, others likely remained silent out of sheer self-preservation. After all, in an industry where your next hit, your next big contract, or your future success can be decided by one powerful figure, speaking out can feel like career suicide.

What's clear is that the **music industry itself** acted as a **shield**, allowing Diddy to continue operating in **plain sight**. The glamorous facade of success, the high-energy parties, and the A-list collaborations masked the **darker reality** behind the scenes. Those who could have intervened chose not to, and in doing so, became part of the system that **enabled Diddy's alleged crimes** to continue for so long.

The allegations against Diddy involve multiple victims, and their stories paint a chilling picture of **manipulation, drugging, and abuse** that spans decades. **Cassie Ventura**, one of the first to come forward, recounted years of **physical violence, sexual coercion**, and psychological manipulation. Diddy reportedly beat her, dragged her down hallways, and forced her into **degrading sexual acts** while under the influence of drugs.

But Cassie's story is just the tip of the iceberg. Several other women, many choosing to remain anonymous, have shared similarly terrifying experiences. One victim, using the pseudonym **Jane Doe**, described being invited to a glamorous party with promises of career opportunities, only to be drugged with **GHB** and wake up with **bruises, bite marks**, and no memory of the night's events. Other women recounted being forced into sexual situations while incapacitated, with Diddy reportedly filming these acts without their consent, using the footage for later **blackmail**.

Patterns of control emerge clearly from the testimonies. Victims were frequently lured into Diddy's orbit with the allure of fame, only to be trapped in a cycle of **abuse and exploitation**. Drugs were a common tool of control—victims were often given powerful substances to ensure their compliance and submission. **Freak-off parties** were not just wild celebrity gatherings, but events orchestrated to degrade and dominate women.

These allegations stretch back as far as the **1990s**, suggesting that Diddy's behavior has been systemic and ongoing for decades. Many women describe **waking up disoriented**, realizing they had been assaulted, and yet finding themselves powerless to speak out, afraid of the consequences.

The Challenge of Speaking Out

FOR DIDDY'S VICTIMS, **fear of retaliation** was a constant barrier to speaking out. His extensive influence in the music industry made him a powerful figure to challenge, and those who attempted to leave or reveal his abuses often faced **intimidation tactics**. Stalking and direct **threats** were reportedly common, and in some cases, even **family members** of the victims were targeted. Diddy allegedly used **hidden footage** of sexual acts from his infamous "freak-off" parties as **blackmail**, ensuring his victims remained silent and trapped in his control.

For these women, the consequences of going against someone as powerful as Diddy weren't just personal—they were professional. Many hesitated to come forward, knowing full well that their careers could be ruined by defying him. The entertainment industry has a history of **ostracizing** those who challenge powerful figures, and victims feared not only public **backlash**, but also being blacklisted from future opportunities. This fear kept many in the shadows, unable to break free from Diddy's grip or tell their stories.

Those who did come forward, like **Cassie**, faced long, grueling **legal battles**. Beyond fighting for justice, they had to fight to reclaim their narratives, battling both the trauma they had endured and the **public scrutiny** that comes with accusing someone as high-profile as Diddy. It took immense courage for these women to speak out, knowing that the road to justice would be paved with threats, intimidation, and legal challenges. Despite the enormous risks, their voices are finally being heard, shining a light on **decades of abuse** hidden behind Diddy's celebrity persona.

The allegations against **Diddy** (Sean Combs) are wide-ranging, spanning over two decades and involving numerous victims. These cases reveal disturbing patterns of **physical, sexual, and psychological abuse**, much of which was reportedly carried out under the guise of industry parties and intimate relationships.

Cassie Ventura

ONE OF THE MOST HIGH-profile victims, Cassie Ventura, who dated Diddy for over a decade, has publicly shared stories of **relentless abuse**, both physical and psychological. She claimed that Diddy often **beat her** and forced her into **sexual acts with male prostitutes** at his infamous "freak-off" parties. Diddy allegedly recorded these encounters and used the footage to **blackmail her** into silence. Cassie also described an incident where Diddy punched her repeatedly in the face after she spoke to another man, later forcing her into a hotel room to "recuperate" for days while forbidding her from attending social events. The psychological manipulation extended to **stalking and threats**, ensuring she remained under his control for years

Adria English

A former porn star named **Adria English** (also known as Omunique) filed a lawsuit in 2024, accusing Diddy of **sex trafficking**. English detailed how she was groomed to engage in sex acts at Diddy's parties. She also claimed that Diddy coerced her into having sex with famous figures like jeweler **Jacob Arabov**, rewarding her with money for her compliance. After attempting to leave, English alleges she was **blackballed** from the industry

Derrick Lee Cardello-Smith

In a highly publicized case, **Derrick Lee Cardello-Smith**, an incarcerated man, won a $100 million judgment against Diddy after accusing him of **drugging and raping** him at a party in 1997. Cardello-Smith claimed that Diddy spiked his drink, causing him to pass out, only to wake up and find that Diddy had sexually assaulted him. The incident highlights the scope of Diddy's alleged predatory behavior, extending beyond women to include male victims

Dawn Richard

Dawn Richard, a former member of Diddy's group **Danity Kane**, also filed a lawsuit accusing him of **sexual, physical, and verbal abuse**. Richard described multiple instances where Diddy physically assaulted both her and Cassie. She recounted a disturbing incident in which Diddy threw a **scalding pan of eggs** at Cassie during a dinner, followed by an attempt to choke her. Richard also witnessed underage girls being brought to Diddy's parties, where they were given drugs and then exploited(
Rodney 'Lil Rod' Jones

Rodney 'Lil Rod' Jones, a music producer, added his voice to the growing list of victims, accusing Diddy of **sexual harassment** and **unwanted groping**. Jones stated that Diddy repeatedly subjected him to **unwanted sexual advances** and pressure to engage in sexual activity, making him another male victim of Diddy's predatory behavior.

Numerous other women and men, often using pseudonyms, have filed lawsuits accusing Diddy of similar behavior, involving **drugging**, **sexual assault**, and **intimidation**. Some victims described being confined for days after violent incidents to "recover," highlighting the extent of control Diddy wielded over his victims.

In **September 2024**, the world of hip-hop and entertainment was rocked when **Sean "Diddy" Combs** was **indicted** on a slew of serious criminal charges. These included **racketeering, sex trafficking by force, fraud, and coercion**, as well as **transportation for prostitution**. This indictment marked a pivotal moment in the long-unfolding saga of Diddy's alleged abuses, revealing how deeply his **corporate empire**, including **Bad Boy Records** and the **Combs Enterprise**, was intertwined with these heinous activities.

The **racketeering conspiracy charge** is particularly significant, as it encapsulates a wide array of criminal acts Diddy allegedly orchestrated through his business entities. Much like the organized crime syndicates of old, Diddy is accused of running his operation with **precision and secrecy**, using his vast influence and wealth to cover up **decades of illegal activity**. The charges lay bare how his empire may have acted as a **front for sex trafficking, drug distribution, forced labor**, and even **witness tampering**—all hidden under the glamorous façade of a successful music mogul.

But the most disturbing allegations are centered around Diddy's infamous **"freak-off" parties**, which, according to the indictment, were **elaborate and highly orchestrated events** where women were allegedly drugged, coerced, and forced into **performing sexual acts**. These gatherings were not just wild celebrity parties; they were allegedly **predatory environments** designed to exploit women, with Diddy at the center of the abuse. Many of the victims, the indictment claims, were too incapacitated to consent, and, to add another layer of horror, these events were often **recorded without the women's knowledge**, further ensuring Diddy's control over them through **blackmail**.

The scale of these accusations has inevitably drawn comparisons to other infamous cases involving powerful men who used their wealth and connections to shield their criminal behavior. Like **Jeffrey Epstein** and **Harvey Weinstein**, Diddy allegedly relied on his **status and influence** within the entertainment industry to silence his victims and cover his tracks. For years, victims were too scared to come forward, fearing **retaliation** not only from Diddy but also from his vast network of **associates** who helped facilitate his actions.

The indictment outlines how Diddy used his **corporate resources and personal wealth** to protect himself from exposure, paying off witnesses, **intimidating those who dared to speak out**, and employing a team of **loyal associates** who helped cover up his crimes. These associates, including **security teams, assistants**, and **high-level executives**, allegedly played key roles in ensuring that Diddy's actions went undetected for years. They helped organize the logistics of his criminal enterprise, from **arranging transportation for victims** to **stockpiling drugs** used to incapacitate them, while Diddy continued to present himself as a charismatic, untouchable figure in the public eye.

What makes this case particularly explosive is the detailed nature of the allegations. The indictment includes chilling descriptions of **physical abuse**—from Diddy **punching and kicking** victims to **throwing objects** at them in violent outbursts. It also reveals a pattern of **emotional manipulation** and **psychological torment**, with Diddy allegedly controlling every aspect of his victims' lives, making them feel powerless to escape his grasp.

As with Epstein and Weinstein, this case has shed light on the dark side of fame and power, showing how the glitz and glamour of success can hide **monstrous behavior**. Diddy's indictment exposes not just the actions of one man, but the **toxic culture of silence and complicity** that enabled him to carry out these acts for so long. If convicted, Diddy faces the possibility of **more than 20 years** in prison, a stunning fall from grace for a man who once stood at the pinnacle of the music and entertainment worlds.

The upcoming trial promises to be a legal and cultural reckoning, one that will likely draw even more **high-profile names** into the spotlight as witnesses, collaborators, and perhaps even co-conspirators. The world is watching as one of the most powerful men in the entertainment industry is finally being held accountable for his alleged crimes.

Courtroom Drama

THE LEGAL PROCEEDINGS against **Diddy** have already started with a **dramatic flair**, beginning with his **arrest at a Manhattan hotel**. The spectacle only intensified when Diddy, maintaining his innocence, swiftly entered a **not guilty plea**. His defense is being led by **Marc Agnifilo**, a high-profile attorney known for representing clients in similarly high-stakes cases. Almost immediately, Diddy's legal team began to **challenge the prosecution's case**, setting the stage for what promises to be an **explosive legal battle**.

The trial has captured the public's attention for multiple reasons, not least of which is the potential involvement of **celebrity witnesses**. According to the indictment, several individuals who were present at Diddy's notorious parties or worked closely with him may be called to **testify under oath**. This could include former **collaborators, party attendees, employees**, and even fellow industry figures who may have been **privy to illegal activities**. As a result, there's significant speculation about who might be forced to **take the stand**, and what secrets could be exposed during the trial. With the prospect of celebrities being subpoenaed, the courtroom is set to become a hotbed of **intense revelations**.

This situation has also sparked widespread public interest and a range of reactions. For some, the news has come as a shocking betrayal—**Diddy**, a cultural icon for decades, is now facing accusations that paint a deeply troubling picture. For others, there is skepticism, as some industry insiders and fans question the motivations behind the accusations and the credibility of the charges.

Amid the courtroom drama, **celebrities** and **industry figures** are coming under scrutiny. Their potential involvement, knowledge of the events, or even **complicity** in Diddy's alleged criminal activities is raising significant questions. As the trial unfolds, the courtroom drama promises to draw even more attention as **testimonies from insiders** could reshape public perception of both Diddy and those around him.

The buzz around who might testify and what they might reveal has only grown louder, making it clear that this case will have **far-reaching implications** for the entertainment industry. This is more than just a legal case—it's a cultural moment that could force an industry to reckon with the **abuses of power** that have been long ignored or swept under the rug.

The Prosecution's Evidence

THE PROSECUTION'S CASE against **Diddy** rests on a wide array of **physical and testimonial evidence** that paints a damning picture of his alleged crimes. During **raids** on his properties, **federal agents** uncovered a trove of disturbing items that they claim were directly linked to his criminal activities. Among the most incriminating evidence were **videos** of Diddy's notorious "freak-off" parties. These tapes allegedly capture women, often drugged and incapacitated, being forced to engage in **sexual acts**, with some unaware they were being filmed. Prosecutors argue that these videos were not only used to **control** the women but also served as a method of **blackmail** to keep them silent.

In addition to the videos, agents seized **narcotics**, including **cocaine** and **oxycodone**, which were allegedly used to incapacitate victims. The **more than 1,000 bottles of baby oil and lubricant** discovered during the raid were said to be used during the abuse, adding to the disturbing nature of the "freak-off" events. Even more concerning, **weapons**, including **AR-15 rifles with defaced serial numbers**, were found on the premises. Prosecutors argue that these firearms were used to **intimidate and threaten** victims and potential witnesses, ensuring their silence through fear and the ever-present threat of violence.

Beyond the physical evidence, **testimonies from multiple victims** are a central pillar of the prosecution's case. Several women have come forward to provide **detailed, first-hand accounts** of the abuse they endured at Diddy's hands. These testimonies include allegations of **physical violence, coercion**, and **sexual assault** during events orchestrated by Diddy and his associates. Victims have described being drugged, waking up with **no recollection** of the events, and later learning they had been recorded and manipulated into silence.

The prosecution also claims to have evidence of **bribery attempts**, with Diddy allegedly offering money and other favors in exchange for **witnesses' silence**. Some of these victims, afraid of the power Diddy wielded both in the industry and personally, initially accepted bribes but have since come forward to expose the full extent of his coercive tactics.

Together, the combination of **seized physical evidence** and **victim testimonies** paints a powerful narrative for the prosecution, suggesting that Diddy's criminal activities were not only carefully orchestrated but also protected by a network of fear, intimidation, and manipulation.

Diddy's Defense Strategy

IN RESPONSE TO THE serious charges laid against him, **Diddy's defense team** has crafted a strategy aimed at **discrediting the victims** and **challenging the narrative** of abuse. At the heart of their defense is the argument that the **sexual activities** at Diddy's infamous **freak-off par-**

ties were **consensual** and that the victims are now coming forward with false claims for **financial gain**. This tactic is typical in high-profile cases where the accused party has significant wealth and influence, and it centers on the idea that the victims are motivated by the prospect of a **financial settlement** rather than seeking justice.

Diddy's **legal team**, led by **Marc Agnifilo**, has made it clear that they intend to **attack the credibility of the witnesses**. This approach will likely involve highlighting **inconsistencies in their stories** and suggesting that their testimonies may have been influenced by the possibility of **media attention** or monetary rewards. By casting doubt on the victims' motives and **questioning their integrity**, Diddy's defense hopes to create enough uncertainty in the jury's mind to **undermine the prosecution's case**.

In addition to challenging the specific allegations, Diddy's defense team is expected to lean heavily on his **public persona** as a **self-made mogul and philanthropist**. They will argue that Diddy, known for his charitable work and family-oriented image, is being **unfairly targeted** by individuals seeking to capitalize on his wealth and fame. By emphasizing his contributions to the **music industry and his philanthropic efforts**, his lawyers will attempt to shift the focus away from the allegations and paint a picture of a **man of integrity** who is being **mischaracterized**.

Moreover, Diddy's team is expected to push the narrative that he has been **cooperative with the investigation**, presenting him as someone with **nothing to hide**. His lawyer has already stated that Diddy is looking forward to **clearing his name in court**, portraying him as a victim of **unjust accusations**. This strategy will also aim to show that Diddy's high-profile status has made him an easy target for people hoping to profit off his misfortune.

These **legal battles** are set to be drawn out, with many **twists and turns** as the trial progresses. Given the complexity of the case and the **explosive nature of the accusations**, it is expected that **more evidence and testimonies** will surface, potentially implicating **other figures** in the music industry. As Diddy's defense unfolds, the court proceedings will likely become a battleground of **reputation, influence, and public perception**, with both sides pulling no punches in their fight for justice.

Media Frenzy

THE **media coverage** of **Diddy's indictment** has been nothing short of explosive, capturing headlines across the globe. Major news networks like **CNN**, **NBC**, and **The New York Times** have dedicated significant airtime to the legal proceedings, breaking down the charges, key moments in the courtroom, and the broader implications of the case. At the same time, **tabloids** and social media platforms have leaned into the more **sensational** aspects of the story, with particular focus on the shocking details of the infamous **"freak-off" parties** that have become central to the allegations. These platforms have latched onto the most lurid elements, including the alleged use of **drugs, hidden cameras**, and **violent coercion**, making this one of the most talked-about scandals in recent years.

The case has drawn **inevitable comparisons** to other high-profile celebrity scandals, particularly those of **R. Kelly** and **Harvey Weinstein**. Like these two men, Diddy is facing charges that go far beyond personal misconduct. The **sex trafficking** and **coercion** charges against him point to a broader, systemic abuse of power, and much like the R. Kelly and Weinstein cases, Diddy's trial is being framed as part of a **cultural reckoning** with the way **fame and influence** have been used to exploit vulnerable individuals, especially women, within the entertainment industry.

As in those previous cases, the **media frenzy** around Diddy's trial is not just about the allegations themselves but also about the broader cultural conversations they have sparked. Coverage in publications like **The Guardian** and **Rolling Stone** has delved into the **power dynamics** in play, examining how someone like Diddy, with his immense **wealth, status, and connections**, could allegedly operate for years without facing serious legal repercussions. This trial has become a symbol of the ongoing debate about how deeply **abuse is embedded** in the entertainment world, echoing the **#MeToo movement** that has already brought down other giants.

While major outlets have aimed for in-depth analysis and contextual coverage, **tabloids** have taken a predictably different approach. They've zoomed in on the **most shocking details**—the drugs, the **1,000 bottles of baby oil**, the alleged **underage victims**, and the **celebrity guests** who attended these now-infamous parties. This sensationalist coverage fuels the public's fascination with the case, making it not only a legal spectacle but also a **gossip sensation**, with every detail scrutinized and dissected by an insatiable media machine.

On **social media**, the case has taken on a life of its own. Hashtags like **#DiddyTrial** and **#MuteDiddy** have gained traction, with users weighing in on every development, often calling for justice for the victims. Twitter, Instagram, and TikTok have become battlegrounds for public opinion, with some defending Diddy, claiming he is the victim of a smear campaign, while others have aligned with the victims, demanding that **Diddy be held accountable** for decades of alleged abuse. In many ways, this mirrors the social media movements that arose during the R. Kelly and Weinstein cases, as the public calls for the entertainment industry to reckon with its **complicity** in allowing powerful men to act with impunity.

THE P DIDDY CASE – FROM MOGUL TO MONSTER

This media frenzy has been instrumental in shaping the **public narrative** surrounding the case. Diddy, once celebrated as a trailblazing figure in hip-hop, now finds his image deeply tarnished, with his legacy hanging in the balance. For years, his public persona was that of a **charismatic mogul**, a man who could throw lavish parties and create business empires while maintaining an aura of control and cool confidence. Now, the media has turned the spotlight on a very different side of Diddy—one marked by **violence, manipulation**, and **exploitation**. As the trial unfolds, the media continues to frame the story as a **fall from grace**, a tragic unraveling of a figure once deemed untouchable.

In this media whirlwind, comparisons to the **#MeToo movement** loom large. The coverage reflects a growing societal recognition that **abuse of power** in the entertainment world must be exposed and confronted, no matter how powerful or beloved the individual may be. For Diddy, the media narrative is clear: this trial is about much more than the allegations themselves. It is about what happens when the bright lights of fame are turned inward to reveal the darkness behind the glamour.

Oh, how the mighty fall—and when they do, it's fascinating to watch everyone else try to sidestep the wreckage. The **Diddy scandal** has sent **Hollywood's elite** scrambling for their publicists' speed dial, trying to figure out whether to **speak out, stay silent**, or maybe just vanish into thin air altogether. In a world where one wrong comment could make you tomorrow's headline, the responses—or lack thereof—are telling.

Strategic Silence: The Ghosts of Hollywood

FIRST, LET'S TALK ABOUT the **masters of silence**—celebrities who've managed to remain spectacularly quiet amid the storm. Heavyweights like **Jay-Z** and **Jennifer Lopez**, both of whom have extensive ties to Diddy, have been keeping their lips sealed tighter than a Grammy after-party guest list. Why? Well, it doesn't take a PR genius to figure out that when the guy who helped you rise to fame is suddenly accused of running a **criminal enterprise** involving **sex trafficking** and **coercion**, the last thing you want is to have your name linked to his downfall. It's as if they're all collectively saying, "Diddy who?" while quietly purging their Instagram feeds of old party pics with him.

But of course, this isn't the first time **Jay-Z** or **J.Lo** have had to navigate a friend's public implosion. Jay-Z has his own experience of dodging the fallout of celebrity scandals, from distancing himself during the fallout of **R. Kelly's** accusations to publicly sidestepping the chaos surrounding **Kanye West's** repeated stumbles. And Jennifer Lopez? She's weathered storms of her own, from her high-profile marriages to her own **PR nightmares**. It's clear: their silence isn't a lack of opinion—it's a carefully curated **masterclass in damage control**.

50 Cent: King of the Trolls

AND THEN, OF COURSE, there's **50 Cent**, who took one look at the headlines and thought, "Here's my moment!" With a feud that's spanned **years, 50 Cent** has never shied away from taking shots at Diddy. And oh boy, has he had a field day with this one. On social media, 50 has been ruthlessly trolling Diddy, using everything from memes to sarcastic jabs to throw shade at his long-time rival. It's hard to tell if 50 Cent has a folder of pre-made Diddy-insults just waiting for a moment like this, but either way, he's practically gleeful as he trolls Diddy's very public tumble. For him, this isn't just about the allegations—it's the perfect excuse to air all his grievances with Diddy while simultaneously collecting social media clout.

What's wild is that 50 Cent's trolling doesn't stop at humorous jabs; it's strategic. He's been using this scandal as a platform to highlight his own brand—subtly inserting himself into the conversation as both commentator and critic. While some might think 50's approach is a bit tasteless given the gravity of the accusations, his fans? They're eating it up, because in the court of **public opinion**, who doesn't love a good celebrity roast?

LL Cool J: The Diplomat

NOW, IF **50 Cent** is the king of trolls, then **LL Cool J** is the **Switzerland** of the music world—neutral, diplomatic, and with just the right touch of empathy. When asked about Diddy's legal woes, LL played it cool (pun intended). He deftly avoided diving into the messy details of the charges, instead focusing on **Diddy's children**. "I feel for his kids," he said, swiftly pivoting the conversation to a topic that wouldn't get him into hot water. A solid move, right? Not too controversial, not too supportive—just enough to acknowledge the situation without putting his own neck on the line. LL is no fool; he knows that there's little to gain from getting too close to this ticking time bomb of a scandal.

It's a classic PR strategy—acknowledge the gravity of the situation without wading too far into the muck. LL's response also hints at a broader trend we've seen in Hollywood recently, where **family sympathy** is often the safest way to comment on a friend's legal crisis without making it worse.

Aubrey O'Day: A Former Protégé Speaks Out

AND THEN THERE'S **Aubrey O'Day**, former member of Diddy's creation **Danity Kane**. O'Day has never been one to shy away from the drama, and this situation is no exception. Her response has been one of **vindication**, finally feeling justified in the years of rumors that swirled around Diddy's behavior. After years of being part of his Bad Boy family, she hinted on social media that the scandal was simply the world catching up to what insiders had whispered about for years. With a sense of justice in the air, O'Day's voice reflects the darker side of celebrity mentorship, where the power dynamics are ripe for exploitation, and the fallout is often severe for the protégés left in the wake.

The Broader Industry Reaction: Shock, Distance, and Fear

ACROSS HOLLYWOOD AND the music industry, the reaction to Diddy's fall has been mixed, to say the least. On the one hand, there's **shock**—not because these kinds of allegations are unheard of in the entertainment world (we've seen this movie before, haven't we?), but because it's **Diddy**. A man who was, for decades, the ultimate symbol of **success**, **wealth**, and **influence**. If **Diddy**—the man behind some of the biggest names in hip-hop and one of the industry's most powerful moguls—could fall this hard, then no one is untouchable.

On the other hand, there's **strategic distancing**. Celebrities and industry figures, especially those who once partied at Diddy's mansions or collaborated with him, are carefully pulling back, probably calling their PR teams for advice on how to navigate this minefield. After all, no one wants to be **guilty by association**, especially when the charges are this explosive. Who wants to answer for attending a party that's now the subject of a federal indictment?

Ultimately, Diddy's indictment has sent a **chill** through the upper echelons of Hollywood and the music world. Some are watching silently, hoping the storm passes without touching them, while others are **trolling, deflecting**, or finding a way to stand up for the victims—all while keeping their own hands clean.

Public perception of **Diddy** has undergone an extraordinary shift as the allegations against him have surfaced. For decades, Diddy was seen as a **hip-hop icon**, a visionary who turned Bad Boy Records into a cultural institution and a **symbol of success** in music, fashion, and business. He was a charismatic mogul who threw lavish parties, brokered multimillion-dollar deals, and stayed at the center of pop culture. However, the allegations of **sexual abuse, coercion, and trafficking** have flipped that narrative on its head, leaving his once untouchable reputation in tatters.

From Mogul to Villain

DIDDY, ONCE A LARGER-than-life figure, is now being **recast** in the public eye. The image of him as a **smooth-talking entrepreneur** and influential party host has been shattered by reports of **manipulation, intimidation**, and **abuse**. The shock waves from the charges have led many to reassess his legacy, with some fans turning on him outright. For others, the juxtaposition between Diddy the **cultural icon** and Diddy the alleged **criminal mastermind** has been jarring, leaving them uncertain about how to feel.

On social media, which has become the central arena for public discourse, Diddy's image has been relentlessly scrutinized. Hashtags like **#MuteDiddy** have begun to **trend**, reminiscent of similar campaigns against **R. Kelly** (#MuteRKelly) and other disgraced figures in entertainment. These movements seek to strip accused celebrities of their cultural power by calling for **boycotts of their music**, businesses, and influence. The voices advocating for justice have grown louder, with many arguing that Diddy's alleged victims deserve to be heard and supported, and that his past achievements should not shield him from accountability.

The Social Media Battleground

AS WITH MANY MODERN controversies, **social media** has become a key battleground for public opinion. Platforms like **Twitter, Instagram**, and **TikTok** have been flooded with posts either condemning Diddy or discussing the broader implications of his case. While some users have been quick to denounce him, others are calling for **due process**, insisting that the public should wait for the legal outcome before passing judgment.

However, the tide seems to be turning against Diddy, especially as more details emerge. The vivid descriptions of the **"freak-off" parties**, allegations of **drugging women**, and the disturbing accusations of **blackmail** have amplified public calls for justice. Supporters of the victims have used these platforms to share stories of **survivor solidarity**, often comparing Diddy's case to those of **R. Kelly, Harvey Weinstein**, and **Bill Cosby**, reinforcing the narrative that **celebrity power can be a dangerous shield** for abusers.

Celebrity Accountability and Wealth Shielding

DIDDY'S TRIAL HAS IGNITED larger conversations about **celebrity accountability** and how **wealth** and **influence** have long acted as shields for those in power. For years, figures like **R. Kelly** and **Weinstein** escaped consequences because of their deep connections and ability to wield their resources against victims who dared to come forward. Diddy, once admired as the epitome of **entrepreneurial success**, is now being held up as another example of how **money, fame, and networks** can allow someone to operate without fear of consequences—at least for a time.

Public debates have also centered on the role of those around Diddy—**his associates, industry partners**, and even the celebrities who attended his notorious parties. As more celebrities distance themselves from Diddy, the question of **complicity** looms large. How much did people know? And why didn't they speak out sooner? These are the kinds of questions that could have a ripple effect across the music industry, forcing more individuals to confront their own role in enabling harmful behavior.

Diddy's Legacy in the Balance

PUBLIC PERCEPTION IS still evolving as the case unfolds, but one thing is certain: **Diddy's legacy is now hanging in the balance.** While some may still see him as a pioneer in the industry, for many, he is increasingly viewed as a **potential predator**—someone who used his fame to **exploit**, **silence**, and **control** others. The outcome of the trial will likely cement this shift in perception, either confirming the accusations and further tarnishing his image or, in the unlikely event of an acquittal, casting a long shadow of doubt over the proceedings.

Ultimately, the scandal has transformed Diddy from a symbol of **unrivaled success** to a cautionary tale of how **unchecked power** and fame can lead to dangerous abuses. His place in history, once glittering and secure, is now deeply uncertain, with the final chapters yet to be written.

Aftermath and the Impact on the Music Industry

Diddy's fall from grace has been nothing short of catastrophic, shaking the foundations of his brand and eroding the empire he spent decades building. Once synonymous with success, luxury, and influence, Diddy's brand is now irreparably tarnished by the allegations of **sexual assault, sex trafficking**, and **racketeering**. The first domino to fall was his lucrative partnership with **Diageo**, which had been the financial backbone of his popular **Cîroc** and **DeLeón** spirits brands. What was once a wildly successful deal, netting Diddy millions, was abruptly severed amid legal battles and growing accusations, causing a significant dent in his wealth and influence.

The separation from **Diageo** marked the beginning of the collapse. With the scandal snowballing, Diddy sold his stake in **Revolt TV**, a network he founded, signaling a clear distancing from his business ventures. The timing of this sale—amid the growing sexual assault allegations—was seen by many as a tactical retreat from a network he had built as a cultural hub for hip-hop and youth media. His fashion label, **Sean John**, has also been left in the dust, as endorsements have dried up, and upcoming projects have been either **canceled** or indefinitely shelved. Once a titan in fashion and music, Diddy's reputation as a mogul has withered, with business partners quickly fleeing from any association with his now-toxic brand.

For a man whose persona was intricately tied to his entrepreneurial success, this fall from grace has been particularly brutal. His estimated net worth, once nearing **$1 billion**, has shrunk dramatically, with many speculating that his financial empire is now in tatters. Diddy's descent marks a sharp contrast from his peak, where he was not only a cultural force but a **business pioneer** who knew how to seamlessly blend music, fashion, and lifestyle into an empire. Now, he is more a cautionary tale of how power and influence can unravel swiftly when deeply hidden abuses come to light.

Broader Implications

THE SCANDAL HAS HAD far-reaching effects beyond Diddy's personal demise. It has **reignited conversations** about **power dynamics** in the music industry, especially how influential figures like Diddy can exploit their positions. The revelations of his alleged coercive behavior, combined with the secrecy surrounding his notorious "freak-off" parties, have drawn **parallels to other major scandals**, including those of **R. Kelly** and **Harvey Weinstein**. Both of these cases illustrated how powerful men, protected by their wealth and status, were able to manipulate, silence, and abuse victims for years.

Diddy's case highlights once again how deeply embedded **sexual exploitation** and **abuse of power** are within the entertainment industry. The #MeToo movement already pulled back the curtain on some of the worst behaviors in Hollywood, but the music industry has largely lagged behind in its reckoning. Diddy's scandal has reopened these discussions, emphasizing that the **toxic culture of silence** and complicity still needs to be dismantled.

This trial has put the music industry on alert, raising important questions about how much **enablers**—from **executives** to **artists**—knew and why they didn't act. The broader industry is being forced to confront its own failures, as Diddy's alleged behavior was an open secret for years, known by many yet shielded by his immense influence. As the scandal continues to unravel, the conversation has begun to shift toward **accountability**, not just for Diddy, but for an entire ecosystem that allowed him to thrive for decades without repercussions.

Impact on Others Involved

THE FALLOUT FROM THE scandal extends well beyond Diddy. His **associates, collaborators, and enablers** have also found themselves in uncomfortable positions, facing public scrutiny for their possible roles in either covering up or ignoring his alleged behavior. High-profile names who were once close to him are now rapidly distancing themselves, with some quietly scrubbing their associations from the public record. These include **celebrities** and **industry executives** who frequented Diddy's infamous parties or worked with him on lucrative projects.

For many, the fear of being associated with Diddy during such a public and damning trial is too much to bear. Several individuals who played key roles in facilitating Diddy's business ventures have also been implicated, either through indirect association or by their silence. Some staff members, including **assistants** and **security personnel**, who were allegedly instrumental in organizing his private events, could face **legal consequences** as investigations continue.

Furthermore, Diddy's fall has sent a chilling message to other influential figures in the entertainment world. For too long, **fame, wealth, and power** have acted as shields, protecting certain individuals from being held accountable for their actions. The rapid unraveling of Diddy's empire serves as a warning to others that the **era of impunity** is coming to an end, and that the industry must change its ways or risk further implosions of its most prominent figures.

In conclusion, Diddy's fall from grace has not only impacted his once-gilded empire but also exposed the deep cracks within an industry that has too often protected its most powerful figures. His scandal marks another critical moment in the continuing conversation about **celebrity accountability**, the misuse of **power**, and the long-lasting effects of **systematic abuse** in the entertainment industry.

Legacy in Ruins - A Tarnished Image

Oh, how the mighty have fallen—right from the penthouse to the courthouse. **Diddy**, once the very embodiment of **hip-hop royalty**, finds himself at the heart of a scandal so deep, not even his designer shades can cover the damage. Let's be honest, for years, Diddy's image was untouchable. He wasn't just the guy behind the beats; he was the guy **everyone wanted to be**. But with these recent allegations, his carefully constructed public persona is crumbling faster than a cookie in hot tea.

For decades, Diddy was celebrated as a **pioneer** in music, a man who turned Bad Boy Records into an empire, not to mention launching **Cîroc** and **Sean John**, and revolutionizing hip-hop culture along the way. He was always "the guy"—the one throwing the most lavish parties, rubbing elbows with celebrities, and making it all look effortless. But now, the headlines aren't about his business acumen or cultural influence. Nope, now he's being compared to the likes of **Bill Cosby** and **Harvey Weinstein**, and not in a good way.

Much like Cosby, who was once "America's Dad" before his reputation was dragged through the mud, Diddy's legacy is quickly becoming overshadowed by the sheer weight of the allegations against him. What was once a shining symbol of success is now a **cautionary tale**—a reminder that no amount of fame or money can hide the truth forever. His contributions to music? Yeah, they're still there, but good luck finding someone who can talk about them without bringing up his **freak-off parties** or **racketeering charges**. It's as if every Grammy, every business deal, every Billboard hit has been blotted out by the sordid details of his **fall from grace**.

The Cultural Reckoning

Diddy's downfall isn't happening in a vacuum—it's part of a larger **cultural reckoning** that's been sweeping through Hollywood and the music industry, thanks to the **#MeToo movement**. For years, these industries have operated with a twisted understanding of what power means, and Diddy, it seems, played his part in keeping those wheels turning. The allegations against him haven't just added fuel to the fire—they've thrown the whole gas station on it.

You see, the entertainment industry has long been guilty of protecting its most powerful figures, letting them get away with behavior that would send the rest of us straight to jail. But the tide has turned. **Diddy's trial** is now a symbol of what happens when **fame and influence** meet the hard truths of accountability. The music industry, which lagged behind Hollywood's #MeToo reckoning, is finally being forced to confront its own ugly truths. And let's face it, the question on everyone's mind is: **How did we let this happen for so long?**

The conversation is no longer just about Diddy—it's about how **systemic abuse** like this could happen in the first place. Why did it take so long for these stories to surface? Who turned a blind eye? And more importantly, what can be done to prevent this from happening again? Industry insiders are now scrambling to rewrite the rules, establishing **zero-tolerance policies** for sexual harassment and abuse, and pushing for reforms that might finally bring some real **accountability** to a world that's spent too long hiding in the shadows.

The Road Ahead

But now, the million-dollar question: Can **Diddy** come back from this? Could he possibly stage a comeback in the years to come, or is he headed for permanent **celebrity exile**? Well, if the playbook of other disgraced celebrities is anything to go by, there might be a sliver of hope for him—albeit a very slim one.

Take **Mel Gibson**, for example. The man was basically written off after a series of highly publicized rants, but with a carefully managed PR campaign and some time out of the spotlight, he managed to claw his way back. Diddy might be eyeing that same strategy, hoping that with time, the public will have a short memory and be willing to give him another shot. But here's the thing: **times have changed**. The public's tolerance for these kinds of scandals has all but evaporated, and the cases against Diddy are far more severe than a few offensive remarks. We're talking about allegations of **coercion, trafficking**, and **decades of abuse**—that's not something you can brush under the rug with a heartfelt apology tour.

Even if Diddy escapes **legal conviction**, the court of public opinion is another beast entirely. He may try to lay low, launch a quiet PR campaign, or even rebrand himself, but it's hard to imagine the public embracing him the way they once did. The road ahead looks grim, and any attempt at rehabilitation would be met with extreme skepticism. The industry, too, will be cautious—who wants to risk their reputation by backing a man whose name is now synonymous with exploitation?

Diddy's legacy, once a shining beacon of success, now teeters on the brink of total **collapse**. Whether he'll be able to salvage any part of it remains to be seen, but one thing is clear: the days of **Diddy the untouchable mogul** are well and truly over.

In writing this book, I set out to explore the complex and often uncomfortable intersection of **fame, power**, and **responsibility** in an industry that has long thrived on excess and indulgence. The story of **Sean "Diddy" Combs**—from his rise as a cultural icon to the staggering allegations that now overshadow his legacy—is one that forces us to confront deeper truths about the world of celebrity. It's a world where success can often come at an unimaginable cost, where **talent and influence** can be wielded as weapons, and where the lines between **consent, control**, and **abuse** can blur dangerously.

This book is not just about Diddy's fall from grace—it's about what his story represents. It's about how we, as a society, have allowed individuals with immense power to exploit it unchecked for so long. The revelations in Diddy's case are emblematic of a larger reckoning, one that has slowly but surely arrived for other figures in entertainment. But it also begs the question: how many others are out there? How many more stories like this are waiting to be told?

As we move forward, it's clear that the old ways of sweeping things under the rug are no longer tenable. **The music industry**, like Hollywood, must take a hard look in the mirror and face its own complicity in allowing these abuses to continue. And for all of us who consume this culture, there's an equally important task at hand: demanding more from our icons, our heroes, and our institutions. Because in the end, the pursuit of fame and fortune should never come at the cost of **human dignity**.

Thank you for joining me on this journey of discovery and accountability. Together, we can strive for a future where **justice, integrity**, and **true responsibility** replace the shadows of manipulation and silence.